Sorry To Hear About Your Dog

By: Colleen Hollis

Illustrated and digitized by Colleen Hollis
Copyright © 2024 Colleen's Children Line Inc. Ltd.
Publisher: Colleen's Novels Inc. Ltd.
ISBN: 978-1-964768-03-8

Not just how to care for an animal, or how to clean up after it.

Your fur-ever friend can also teach you that a bond as strong as the one between you and your dog can never be broken.

How else do you explain that your pal knew whether you were sad or sick, happy or just ready for a nap.

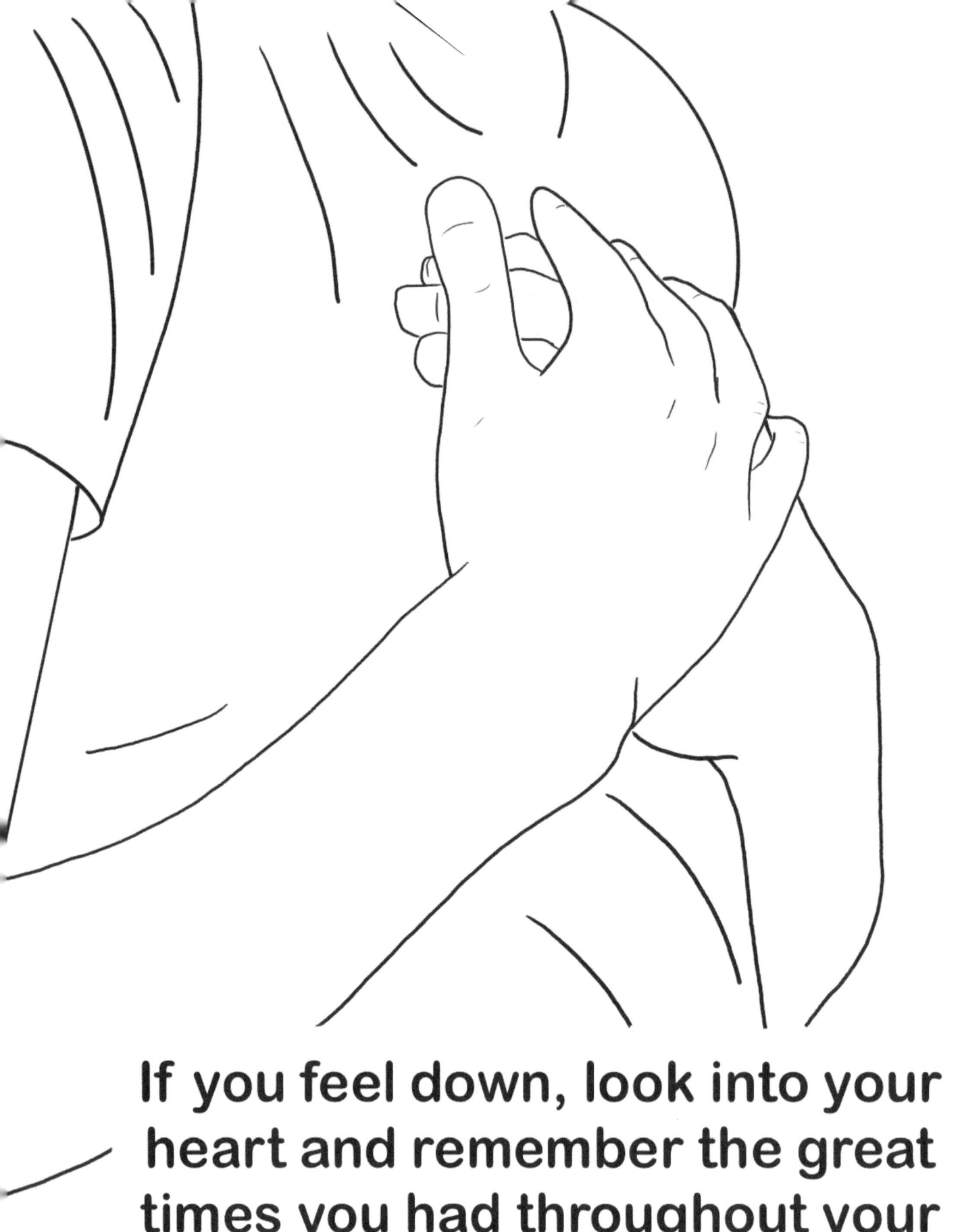

If you feel down, look into your heart and remember the great times you had throughout your friendship.

All the games of catch while playing in the park.

Not to mention the countless hours of laughing and running after each other in the yard.

By being willing to remember these moments, you honor your fur-ever friend.

We know how much you love
your fur-ever friend.

We also realize how much you came to depend on your fur-friend.

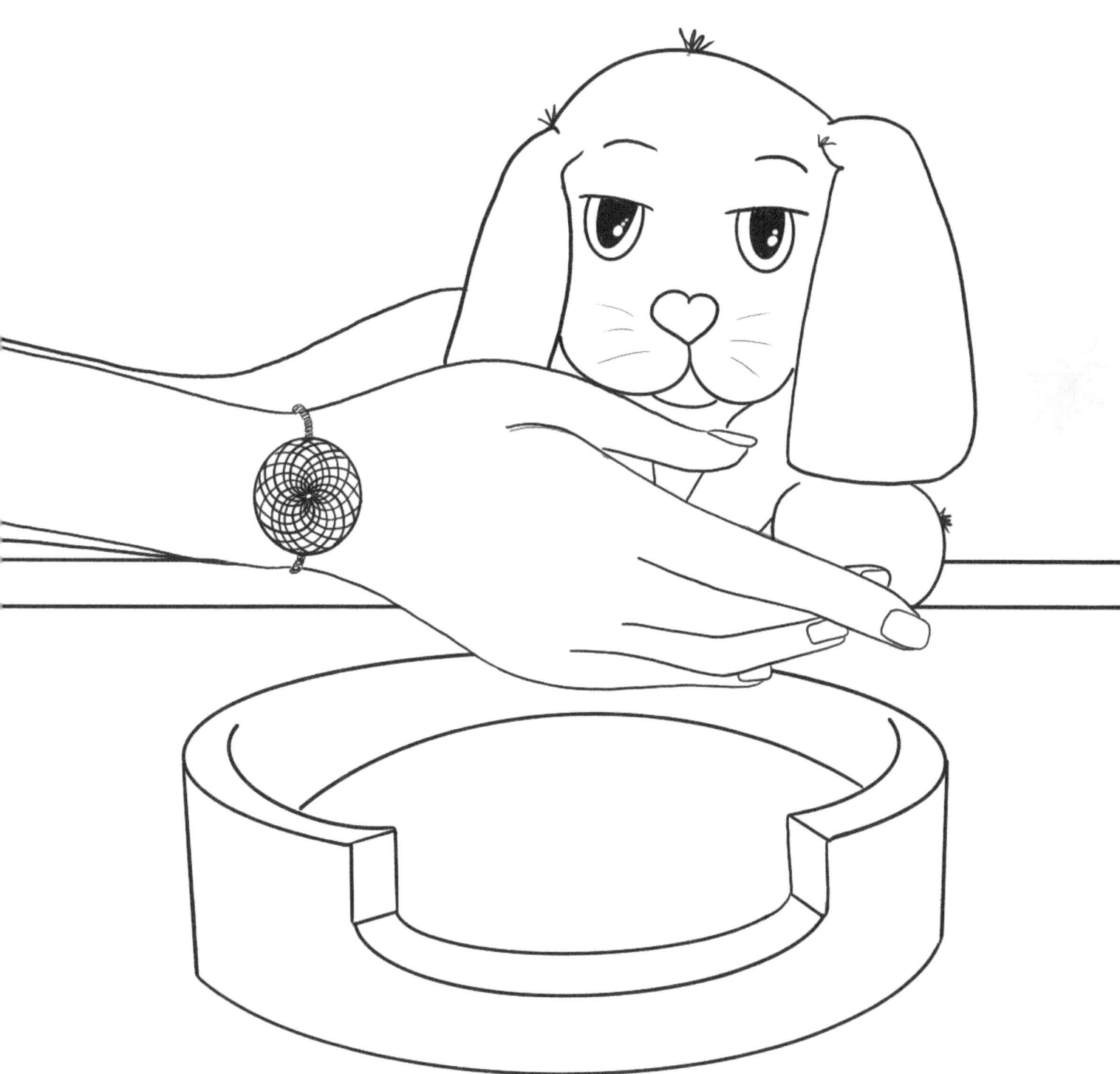

Wherever you were found,
there was your pal.

If you need to talk, you always have our support.

It may be difficult as you face the upcoming days and months without your pal.

The memories may bring tears now, but as time passes the tears will turn into smiles as you think of your fur-ever friend with love.

Recalling the adventures that you had, with time, the pain will get easier.

Maybe even recall a bit of the mischief you two got into from time to time, that will also help.

Please feel free to discuss how you are feeling at any time.

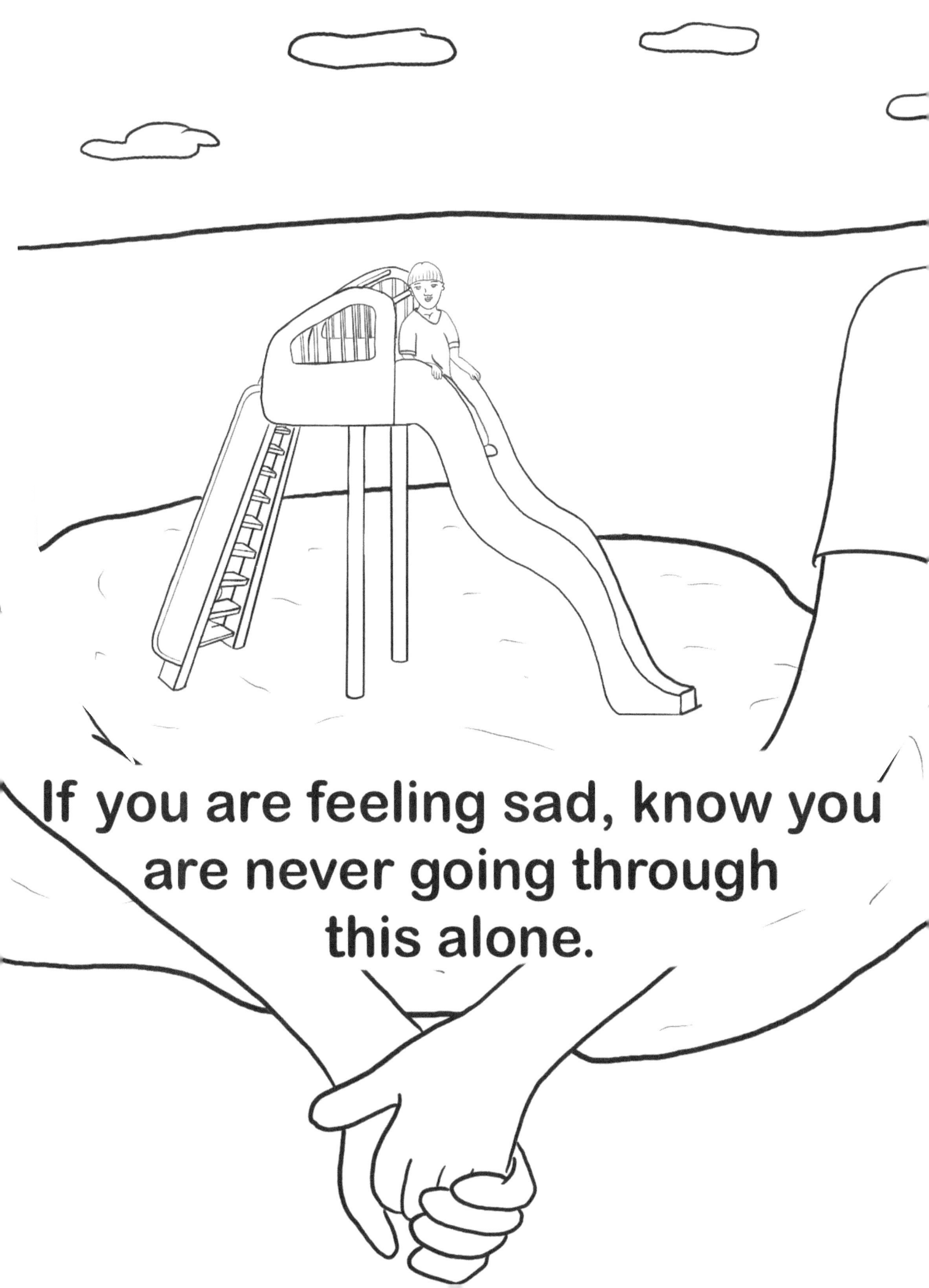

If you are feeling sad, know you are never going through this alone.

We are here to help however we can.

Even if all you need is a hug while you sit thinking of your friend, I'll be here.

Thank you for all the hard work you put into taking such good care of your fur-friend.

We are so proud of you.

You are loved forever and always.

Love, _____

Friend's Facts

Friend's Name:_____

Friend's Age:_____

Friend's Favorite Food/s:_____

_____

Friend's Favorite Activity:_____

_____

Friend's Favorite Toy/s: _____

_____

Friend's Favorite Person/s:_____

_____

Feel free to write a little note, or share a memory or two.

Sorry To Hear About Your Dog, is one of the books in the children's line from Colleen's Bereavement Line For Children. Colleen's Bereavement Line for Children is aimed to assist in the healing process of children that find themselves navigating the loss of a loved one or pet. Sorry To Hear About Your Dog focuses specifically on those with a dog companion. A name can be added to the beginning of the book, while in the back of the book there is space to write memories about the fur-ever friend. Followed by a page for "Friend Facts" that can be filled in for a more personal feel.

All animal books in the series are interactive as well, they are in a coloring book format. Art has been shown as a useful tool that can aid in the healing process.